Lesbian First Times: 15 Women Share Their First Time Sexual Experiences with Women

Angie Rose

Table of Contents

Part I
Get Ready

Introduction

Lesbian First Times is a collection of 15 women detailing their first time sexual experiences with a woman. The accounts of their first sexual experience with another woman are hot, tantalizing, with nothing being held back. Asked by author Angie Rose to provide as much detail as possible, they disclosed every sexy detail in their recounts of these intensely intimate experiences.

You are about to uncover sexy girl on girl stories:

Amber in Amsterdam

Dana's Dressing Room First

Alexa and Summer's First

Simone's Massage

In Bed with Olivia

Marissa and the Photographer

Jenn the Artist

Dominique at My Beach House

Kylie and Noelle

Roommates

Softball Playing

All-Girl School Hook Up

Camping with Sharon

Sierra in the Dorm

Hot Soccer Players

In *Lesbian First Times*, you will hear from real lesbians and read about their real first time lesbian experience stories. Exciting, explicit, and tempting, this book is sure to please and is refreshingly real!

Amber in Amsterdam

It's ridiculously hot and I can't even breathe. I do not have an AC here in my house. It's 95 degrees right now where I live in Palm Springs, California. I took three cold showers today and it's only the afternoon. The topic I'm going to talk about with you today is very hot and steamy as well. I'm going to tell you about my first lesbian sexual experience...

I remember this girl. She was beautiful. She was smart, she was sexy, and she was gay. This was back when I still lived in Amsterdam. Before meeting her, I had kissed girls before but nothing else. I always had boyfriends. I always told myself I was straight. I did fool around with girls but it never led anywhere. It was too young; I was too scared. It was kind of just like play to me.

Then, I met this girl and she was so hot and so beautiful. Her name was Amber. She liked me and she was so bold when she would speak to me. With a hot accent, she said "I think you're hot and I think you like me too so I think we should get together." I said "You know I have boyfriend." She would be like "No, that's gonna change, there is no way you're going to have boyfriends."

At some point, she invites me to a party. We had a few drinks. The sexual tension was so insane I felt like I couldn't even sit next to her. I felt like, if I sat next to her she would hear my heart race because it was so fast and so loud.

I remember, one thing led to another, and we ended up in the back room of the house we were partying at and in the same bed. She kissed me and I kissed her back. I remember that was the first kiss where I felt like this might lead somewhere else. I thought we might end up doing something much more than kiss. I was so nervous. I felt like I forgot how to kiss in that moment but I could tell she was so into it.

It felt like a movie, even though it sounds cliché. It felt like there were fireworks when we were kissing and I felt like I could breathe for the first time in my life. It was so amazing.

Before that night (the evening before I ended up in bed with her) I kind of figured something might happen because my boyfriend was away and I was able to do whatever I wanted to do. I was convinced even more when she was like "We're gonna do it. It's going to happen for you today." It was such a turn on how confident she was and how bold she was with me.

I wanted her so much but I remember worrying that I wouldn't know what to do. I thought "What do I do?" and "Where do I touch?" but the more we kissed the more I felt like I knew what to do. All my questions went away.

Amber had a lean, tan body. I gazed at it when we broke away from kissing. I took her in with my eyes. Her body was so responsive to everything I did to her. She pushed my hand slowly with her hand until I could feel her mound. Right away I began rubbing. She still had her thong on so I rubbed for a while we were kissing and breathing so hard almost in sync with each other.

She smelled like coconut tanning oil and I was wet and soaking by the time she was ready to slide her thong off. We pulled it off together and I looked at her gorgeous face with excitement. There was nothing that could stop me from pleasing her.

I realized at that moment that I loved pleasing a woman. I slid my one finger inside her and stroked back and forth, deeper and deeper. She was so wet and so open that she needed more and she told me to slide another in her and you know I did.

I was glad that I had played with myself so much alone because I knew I needed to play with her clit with my thumb while thrusting inside of her with my fingers. We were both so turned on that it felt like it took no time for her to cum all over my hand. She kissed me and then opened her eyes and stared into me.

Then, she turned me over with her toned arms, placed her hands under my ass, and grabbed it while she slid her tongue across my exposed mound and opened up jeans. She pulled them along with my lingerie bottoms down hard. It was then that she proceeded to spread my legs and please me with her entire mouth. I had never felt such big warm lips on my clit in my life. I was so turned on that I came within minutes. I remember feeling her breathe hard onto me when I was finished cumming. She laid her face on my lower stomach and massaged my body with her hands.

Amber's sex opened up my world. It was amazing and beautiful. The connection between us made me throw all of my questions out. I never went back to having sex with men again. She didn't become my girlfriend because she knew I was moving to the U.S. But she opened me up to a new world and I'll never forget her. If she's reading this...I'd love to thank her for the exciting ride.

Sierra in the Dorm

Sierra and I shared a dorm room in college. One night, we were partying and by the time we got to the second party we were already pretty intoxicated. It was around 1 AM and I was ready to go back to the dorms but Sierra said she heard the guy she was talking to would be at this house, so we went.

The house party was crowded. Sierra scanned the first room, and I moved toward the kitchen to find more alcohol. In the kitchen there was a group of guys.

"So, how do you girls know each other?" one of the guys asked.

"We're roommates," Sierra answered, "this is my best friend!" She hugged me, letting her hands fall and rest on my ass. We laughed.

Another guy looked us up and down and asked, "Have you two ever messed around?" He laughed.

"Oh, only every night." Sierra answered in a flirty tone. I blushed, and laughed a little. She was joking but it seemed like she liked saying it for attention.

The guys must have known this was a joke, but one guy asked us to prove it.

All the sudden, Sierra grabbed my face and kissed me. I kissed back. She lowered her left hand to my ass and squeezed. My hands moved from her waist to her hips while she squeezed and smacked my ass playfully. The guys cheered and we separated. I laughed a little nervously.

The guys asked us back to their place, but we agreed we were tired and ready to go back to our dorm. On the walk back, Sierra said "They loved it. Did you see their faces when I kissed you?"

I laughed, "Yeah, they did seem pretty excited. And it was pretty hot."

When we got in our room, we immediately started undressing like we normally would. Usually when Sierra is changing, I sneak a few glances at her body. Tonight I found myself staring.

Her ass was bigger than mine, and I'd always wanted to feel it. It was round and perky and looked so sexy in a thong. She was practically naked now, and I was too. I wanted to get closer to her.

I took my bra off and didn't bother looking for a shirt to sleep in. My nipples were hard and I wanted her to see. Now, more than anything, I wanted Sierra to touch them.

She turned around and so we were facing each other wearing nothing but panties. I smiled at her.

"Why haven't we experimented?" she asked me, "We just made out. We're turned on. Why shouldn't we mess around?" She stared at my tits and I moved toward her.

I let the alcohol take over and I said "I want to be inside of you." She pulled me closer and kissed me hard.

"I'm so horny," she moaned, "oh my God, Fuck me."

We moved to our sofa and I straddled her. I let my pussy grind against her while I kissed and sucked her nipples.

She moaned and slapped my ass leaving imprints.

"Sit on my face," she commanded. I positioned my pussy over her and moved my panties to the side. Her tongue probed my hole and I moaned as I felt it inside of me. Then she started to lick and tease my clit, making me want her even more. I squeezed and played with my own nipples, watching her taste me.

After a minute, I turned my body so we could sixty-nine. She spread her legs wide and I moved her thong to the side so I could eat her out. I felt her moans against my own clit and almost came right then. I gave her pussy a few licks and sucks before sucking on her clit, making her legs shake.

She pulled my panties off of me and kneeled behind me so she could lick me again.. Then she moved back to my clit, and started fingering me. With my ass in the air, she paused for a moment and got something which I quickly realized was a vibrator. She placed it on my clit while she fingered me and licked all around. I came harder than I ever had in my life. She licked me until I couldn't stand it anymore and had to push her away.

Then she laid down on her back and spread her legs for me to finish her off.

I laid between her legs and went straight for her clit. I teased and sucked her clit while adding my middle finger and using my free hand to put the vibrator directly on her clit.

I remember her entire body rose as she came and her breathing almost stopped. She pushed me away and I moved to lay next to her. We were both more than ready to go to sleep.

We said goodnight and climbed into our own beds like normal, and I hoped we would do this again and it did.

Hot Soccer Players

I felt like we had the world's prettiest girl on our soccer team. She had the perfect body for me, and a lot of times I would catch myself staring at her on the field, quick to turn away if she saw me. Ever since the first time I saw her, I had fantasized about her.

Watching her was exactly what I was doing this early Wednesday morning. We planned to travel with the team to the Cup tournament, and it was early in the morning.

Once at the Cup site we set up our sleeping gear in the classroom we had been allocated. My heart skipped a beat when Samantha threw her mattress next to mine, smiling. I wondered why she settled there and not in one of the corners far away, as usual.

We had traveled far to get to the Cup. It was already late when we had settled in, and with a game the next day, we went to bed early. Just before I was about to fall asleep, I felt Samantha's fingers gently stroking me along my arm. It only lasted a few seconds and she stopped just as quickly as she started. I could not be absolutely sure that she really did it on purpose. Despite my doubts I shivered and wanted her to continue, but she did not.

The next day was the first game. I did not think about Samantha's caress the previous night, until she caught my eye during breakfast. She smiled at me. All morning my mind was preoccupied with her.

Later that day, I asked her to take a walk with me. After walking for a while I remember stopping to sit on a bench.
We sat next to each other in silence for a moment and looked at the starry sky. At least she did. I was just too focused on her right thigh touching mine.

We got up and started walking again. We discussed the game. We crossed an open area and reached the start of a path. I turned around to start going back, but stopped suddenly at the entrance to the path.

"What is it, Samantha?" I asked, and turned back to her. She said nothing, just looked at me. I got caught up in her eyes. My heart raced. She took a step closer to me and she let the back of her hand caress my cheek. I held my breath as her face approached mine. I could feel her breath on my lips, and now I would finally get to feel her lips against mine. Then her cell phone rang.

"Damn," she mumbled and answered.

"Hello?"

Days passed on the Cup. We tried to get a moment alone, but there was always someone who ruined it for us. I saw how irritated Samantha became. Matches went very well for us. On Monday we played in the semifinals, unfortunately losing 2-1 after extra time. So on Tuesday we played for third place, and won 2-0. Afterwards came all the euphoria of victory and everyone hugged each other. I held Samantha closely for a long moment as my hands explored her lower back. Before she released me, she let her lips press into my cheek. I shivered.

The following day was the journey home. I was really annoyed because Samantha and I still had not managed to be alone. When we arrived home, it was so unthinkable, that all would surely be back to normal but I wanted whatever was happening between us to continue.

We had not seen each other for several weeks, besides with the team, but she continued to smile sweetly at me. After one workout, I decided to take a shower because I planned to visit some friends afterwards.

Expecting to have the dressing room all to myself, I was very surprised when Samantha followed me in, apparently to shower with me.

"Well, why are you showering here, when usually you're not?" she wondered.

"No, I usually don't. But today I am visiting some friends, so I thought it was better that I shower here and then go there immediately," I replied. "You then, why are you also here?"

"Ha-ha," laughed Samantha. "For the same reason, actually." We laughed. She threw back her hair over her neck and smiled at me again. She stepped out of her clothes and tried to look away as I got out of mine.

We stepped into the shower and I just could not take my eyes off her lean smooth body. When I looked up at her, I blushed, realizing that she knew I was eying her. She looked at me the same way that she had on the Cup trip, when we almost kissed. She took a cautious step toward me. We stood facing each other, with only an inch separating our bodies. Samantha extended her hands and placed them on my shoulders. She then pulled me close and let her lips meet mine. I exploded inside, never imagining this would finally happen.

I pulled her toward me while we kissed. Finally, I got to feel her naked body next to mine. Her hands eagerly caressed my back and thighs, and her hand found the inside of my thigh. My hands stroked her body and quickly found her breast. She groaned as both my hands for the first time fondled her breasts. In response she kissed me harder, and she forced me back against the wet wall.

Her hands caressed my stomach and hips, and slid teasingly on my mound. Suddenly, she cupped her hand between my legs. Her fingers slowly teased my outer lips, then she gently slid a finger along the moist slit of my pussy and up toward my clit. When she finally touched my clit, I moaned being very aroused. She smiled, took my hand, and looked into my eyes.

"Come on," she said, pulled me away, threw our towels on the floor in the middle of the locker room and laid me down.

Her lips met mine again. My hands slid further down and caressed her thigh. She groaned and we rolled onto our sides. Her hands squeezed my breasts, and then went behind my back to pull me next to her. She grazed her lips over my neck and throat, and I could feel my body shaking. I moved my hand to her pussy and gently probed, as she groaned. My touches became more forceful, and she moaned louder and louder, finally screaming in pleasure. I could not believe I was actually doing this with her. I had fantasized about her for so long.

Seeing her pleased made me very excited, and I stopped suddenly to caress her. I saw in her eyes that she understood what I was about to do. I kissed her neck, and she leaned her head back. My kisses walked further down her body. I took my time to kiss her breasts and stomach, before my lips found their way to her mound. I kissed and licked her pussy lips as she moaned with excitement. I finally let my tongue sweep across her clit. Samantha moaned and began to thrust her hips up to my face. My tongue probed and circled her clit fast, and it was not long before she tensed her entire body and screamed while she came. Then her body went limp, in total relaxation, as she opened her eyes and she smiled at me.

I kissed her and felt her hands again on my thighs. Samantha smiled happily and crawled back up to me. Her fingers stroked softly over my cheek and she kissed me.

"I love you," she whispered.

Dana's Dressing Room First

I remember one day back in high school shopping with my friend Dana and leading her into a popular store. We looked through clothes and, after finding a couple of outfits to try on, we headed for the dressing rooms. The dressing rooms were really nice. Each had a solid door and a nice long bench, and were very private. Dana also noticed that no one else seemed to be around, and got to thinking... it would be so hot to mess around right in the dressing room! We had kissed before but nothing else and we wanted each other badly that day.

I entered a dressing room and tried on an outfit. Dana was waiting outside. I opened it to show her outfit. Dana's eyes widened and told me, "You're so beautiful."

I pulled her into the dressing room, shut the door and kissed Dana as I pushed her against the wall. Dana's hands roamed over my body, up and down, everywhere, as she kissed me on the neck and shoulders. She told me how much she had wanted me, but I replied, "We can't. Not in here. Let's go home..."

Dana said no one would know what we were doing if we were quiet, which made us both laugh. Because each knew that they were much too passionate for silent kissing let alone lovemaking.

Dana kissed me again. After more kissing, Dana

unbuttoned my pants and took my hand and put it inside her so I could feel how wet I had made her. When I felt the flood between Dana's legs, I groaned into our kiss. She knew I needed her.

I remember nervously looking around while I started moving my hand against Dana's wet and throbbing pussy. The feeling of my fingers playing through Dana's slippery slit was incredible. I took my hand and pushed under my jeans, sliding my panties to the side so Dana would touch me.

We both became even wetter. It felt like we knew exactly what to do to each other in that moment. At first we each rubbed all around each other's pussy. Then we both started finger fucking the other. We kept as quiet as possible despite the fact that we were so hot for each other. Our hips were thrusting into each other's hands and our mouths were devouring each other. Dana's free hand grabbed my ass and pulled it tighter toward her, and I knew I was going to explode shortly.

She rubbed my clit harder and then fingered me deeper, ordering me to "come with me." We both gasped for breath and kissed frantically, grinding into each other when we felt it coming. Dana told me she was going to come when she felt my pussy grip her fingers tightly, and Dana felt the explosion hit.

After we came, we stood there for a minute, just holding each other as we tried to calm down. I whispered, "We gotta go" as I removed my hand from Dana and then kissed her deeply.

We straightened our clothes while listening whether the coast was clear. We left the dressing room wondering if anyone had heard us.

Alexa's and Summer's First

Alexa was my girlfriend. We'd just started college. I had been with a few women already but had never used a strap-on and Alexa was still a virgin. She hadn't even slept with a man much less a woman. We were in love and she asked me to take her virginity. This is our story (me using a strap- on for the first time and Alexa making love to a woman for the first time).

I remember one night we had together after going to a basketball game. Stumbling back into her room, she turned and we kissed. She took hold of my shirt and unbuttoned it, pulling me with her as she backed towards the bed. She sat on the edge of the bed and ran her hands over my chest as I stood in front of her.

She smiled at that, then unbuttoned my pants and pulled them down. Reaching up and taking hold of my boxer briefs, she released the dildo that I had strapped-on for her, before looking up again.

She laughed, then pulled her top over her head and quickly unhooked her bra to reveal her C-cup breasts. I reached down and ran my fingers over her hard nipples, then let my own shirt fall to the floor, and knelt in front of her.

Pushing her legs apart either side of me, I shuffled forwards on my knees and kissed her stomach. I turned my attention to her breasts, and kissed both nipples, before starting to lick and suck one while I rubbed soft circles over the other with my fingers. She let out a small moan and ran her fingers through my hair, clutching me to her.

Moving my head slightly, I kissed between her breasts, and then slightly lower, and lower again. Kissing down her stomach, I pushed her skirt up around her waist, kissing against her mound through her neon yellow thong. She lay back and raised her legs, allowing me to peel her thong down her legs and off her feet, before she set her legs back down.

I leaned in and ran my tongue along her groove, rewarded by a moan from Alexa. Spreading her lips with my fingers, I searched out her clit with my tongue, drawing another moan as I slowly ran my tongue up and down over it. I licked her soft and slow for a minute or so, before pulling her towards me and pressing my tongue hard against her clit, and starting to speed up.

She let out a moan at that, and reached down to place a hand on my head and held me against her wet pussy. I worked two fingers inside her as I continued to lick and suck her engorged clit, and started to pump them into her tight hole as I tongued her.

Moaning loudly, her hips writhed up and down against my tongue, and she shouted as her breathing quickened "God I'm gonna cum, Fuck me!"

I stood and slid my strap-on dildo between her pussy lips, and she gasped as I plunged it in. Just two thrusts later I felt her pussy walls contract and she squeezed her breasts as her back arched.

I continued to pump my dildo into her soaking wet pussy, thrusting hard as she moaned and gasped. She told me she was cumming and moaned loudly.

I pressed my hips slowly forward into Alexa and resumed a slow rhythm. Her legs were so long wrapped around me. After cumming, she laid there, hand between her legs. I moved in to kiss her again while still inside of her.

Simone's Massage

I had been friends with Simone since junior high. We were both 18 and still seniors in high school when we had a sexual experience together. She identified as gay and I was straight at the time.

I remember her asking me if I would ever hook up with a girl. I said "I don't think I could ever be attracted to a girl." I'm pretty sure Simone saw it as a challenge that I told her I wasn't into girls.

Simone was tall and curved in all the right places with tanned skin and dark hair. She carried herself as if she knew she was beautiful.

One day she asked me if I trusted my body. I asked her what she meant. She asked "I mean do you trust what your body tells you?" She said that I had formed an opinion from thoughts in my head that I couldn't be with a girl and that even though my mind was telling me one thing my body might tell me something different. She asked me, "If your body told you something different would you trust your body?"

I told her that I didn't know and she asked me if I was willing to try. She asked "Are you willing to give your body a chance to tell you what your mind might not yet know?" I said that I wasn't sure but maybe.

She took me to another room in her house. There was a massage table in her parents' spare bedroom with a bed sheet draped over. She asked me if I had ever had a massage. I replied "yes" and she told me "Good, so you will be comfortable undressing for a massage." I smiled and told her to leave while I undressed and got on the table. I made sure to place the sheet over my entire body.

I remember feeling scared and I didn't know what to expect. I loved massage but I found myself more excited than I was just going to the spa. I knew it was because her hands would be on me and that feeling shocked me and made me so nervous.

She knocked gently, asked if I was ready, and I told her she could come in.

She told me "You have complete control. You can stop anything that happens at any moment. Feel free to tell me where you want massaged and where you don't."

I was lying face down on the table with my face in the cushioned cut out. I peeked with one eye and saw Simone had only a zebra print bra on. I smiled but she didn't see me. I remember shaking a bit in anticipation.

She had a bottle of massage oil on the dresser next to the table. I heard her open it up to release some into her hands.

She breathed deeply and began caressing my neck and shoulders.

She said "I am going to use my hands and some light massage oil and will be touching your skin." She asked me if I was okay with that. Of course, I replied yes.

She told me she was going to uncover my back. I swallowed hard and answered yes.

She drew the sheet back slowly, exposing my back. She was careful not to uncover my panties still hidden under the sheet. As she began to rub me down, she told me I was holding a lot of stress and tension in my shoulders and back.

Then she asked me "May I undo the clasp of your bra?"

I remember being silent for a moment. Simone waited patiently. After a minute I answered "Yes."

Gently, she undid the clasp and part the straps. I heard her rub her palms together to warm the oil, and she spread the warmed oil across my skin. Then she slid her thumbs down along my back muscles playing across my warmed skin. Gradually, I started to relax under her hands. She slipped her fingers under the straps of my bra and slid them outwards, very slowly. She asked, "May I slide the straps of your bra out of the way?"

"Yes," I said quietly.

She slid them away and massaged my bare shoulders and neck firmly. This part I remember so distinctly. She let her fingertips brush along the side swell of my breasts as she worked down my arms to my sides. I stiffened a bit but I didn't say a word and at that moment I became wet. She worked down to the narrowing of my waist, letting her fingertips play across the small of my back, dipping just under the edge of the sheet to lightly brush the edge of my panties. She quickly came back up to the top of my back and massaged seductively.

When she gets back down to the small of my back, I am ready for her to go down further. At that point, she transitioned her hands to the sheet and stroked firmly down the outside of my thighs. Her hands continue their transit up the back of my thighs and smoothly over the sheet and swell of my ass. As her hands approached the edge of the sheet, she slipped her fingertips under the sheet edge and played them across the lace top of my panties.

I swear I thought I would have told her to stop but I couldn't. I was too excited and too wet to make her stop.

She continued rubbing my ass with her hands with the sheet still on my lower half. Her open palms caressed my thighs and I relaxed into the sensation. Then, she continued the caress down the length of my firm, long legs.

"May I lift the sheet to work on your legs?" she asked. I remember nodding yes and not being able to speak.

She lifted the bottom of the sheet up and uncovered my feet, calves, and massaged them firmly as she worked her way up. She told me my legs were strong and beautiful.

As her oiled hands stroked and caressed, she worked the sheet up to my thighs, firmly massaging their backs and sides but allowing her fingertips to lightly caress the sensitive skin of my inner thighs. My legs are still close together and while I'm relaxing, I still hold myself tightly. Slowly, the sheet is just covering my panties. She said, "I'd like to move the sheet up higher now, is that okay?"

"Yes," I said.

She lets her hands roam freely over me, down the side of my breast, to my waist, across my ass, down my thigh, back up into my inner thigh. My thighs part incrementally with each pass and she begins rubbing my between my thighs and into my groin. I'm sure she notices the scent of my arousal now that she is so close to me. She rubs gently, then proceeds to rub more firmly. I can hear her breathing hard.

"It's time to turn over onto your back now" she says.

I turn over without hesitation and I allow the sheet to slip off onto the floor. My heart is racing now.

She begins to massage my upper pectoral muscles and down my breasts. She caresses the curves around my sides and then down my ribs. Massaging my stomach, she works the tension out of me while massaging my hips and fronts of my thighs. She follows the ridge of my hips into the tight groin tendons, and my thighs part giving her more access.

"I'd like to remove these now," she says.

I lift my hips in response without a word or hesitation.

She slips the panties down my hips quickly but gently. She resumes massaging the muscles of my upper thighs.

As she works the rest of the stress and tension out of my body, she leans over and breathes a warm breath across my nipple lets her breath out shakily.

"Should I continue?" she asks. I can't keep up the pretense of calm control anymore. I know she can feel the desire in my body.

"Yes," I whisper.

With her palms cupping the outside of my breasts, she allows her thumbs to rise up and brush across both nipples. I arch under her hands and a moan escapes my parted lips. She squeezes lightly and then more firmly.

She moves to stand at the head of the table and drops down so her mouth is right by my ear. "I want to taste you now."

I bite my bottom lip and breathe my consent.

She lightly licks the curve of my ear and then draws my earlobe between her teeth, grazing it gently. I shiver and the goose bumps rise down my arms and breasts. She kisses and licks around my breast.

She darts the tip of her tongue across the sensitive tip of my nipple and it immediately becomes even more aroused and swollen. She sucks the sensitive flesh and flicks the tip of her tongue rapidly over the peak until I moan. She rolls the other nipple between her thumb and forefinger and squeezes gently. My fingers tangle in her as I pull her against me, arching into my mouth.

She slips her hand down and caresses my inner thigh firmly. I can feel the damp heat radiating from my core. She kisses her way down to my stomach as her hand moves up. She pauses and I am silent until finally I whisper, "Yes,"… "Yes".

She slips her fingers into my heated oiled up pussy and rubs me until she I am weak from pleasure.

In Bed with Olivia

My first girl on girl experience was classy. It was in a fast food restaurant in the bathroom! Awesome right? Really not the most romantic but it was very hot. It was one of my best guy friends who asked me to kiss my best friend at the time. I lost it, mainly because I had the biggest crush on her at that time. Our guy friend stared at us and waited for us to hook up. I turned beat red and it felt like months I was standing there. Lucky for me, she made the first move. We made out for what seemed like forever.

But that was just my first girl on girl kissing experience. My first actual sex session with a girl was at my grandmother's house. It was summer and I had almost no supervision. Me and this girl Olivia (whom I had met through some friends of mine) were staying in the spare room. We were partying all night long. Me and Olivia went to bed together after sneaking in the window of the spare room.

We were grinding our pussies together with our underwear still on while making out. She had been with girls before so she went right to rubbing my crotch. She slid my underwear to the side and slipped her fingers right in to me. The slid in with ease so I know I was turned on. She made me cum for the first time in my life.

My grandmother came in the room and we were both naked. She asked us if we heard the screaming outside and asked what was going on. No one was screaming outside. I was screaming in the spare room from the girl going down on me.

Marissa and the Photographer

I'm open about sex. I do a lot of modeling and I've made a career out of it now. I like to play with girls but I mostly have sex with men now or I'll have threesomes. My first lesbian experience was in middle school. Everyone in middle school in my group of friends went through a phase when they would feel bisexual or gay. It was a time to experiment. I had a friend named Marissa who I had my first lesbian experience with. I would go to her house and we were like best friends. Marissa gave me the best full body massages with oil. We messed around a lot. She had really big boobs and I had A cups so I became obsessed with seeing her without a bra on. She was a cute rocker type chick.

We would grab the dildo and vibrator from her parent's bedroom. We would kiss and lick each other. I loved the way her tongue ring felt against my tongue. I can also remember the first time she put her fingers in me. I was still a virgin so I was really tight. She stuck one finger inside of me first and it felt so good. She started to move it in and out of my pussy and I begged her to put another one in. She laid me back on the bed and spread my legs wider then slipped another finger inside of me. She placed her palm face up and bent her fingers and hit my G spot just right. I screamed out in pleasure. She was my first and I'll never forget how good she made me feel.

Another interesting encounter with a woman I had was during big shoot I got to do with a photographer. She is a big photographer in the business. I had just started modeling at the time. We ended up going to a strip club after the shoot. On the way back she was really drunk and she started making out with me. I had always said I wouldn't hook up with a photographer but she was a woman so I felt like it was different. The photographer and I stayed in touch and I went down to see her for a paid gig. It was for a calendar shoot. We went out to a rock concert. Her boyfriend was in a band and we ended up seeing him and then going back (just the two of us) to her house to have sex.

Jenn the Artist

The first time I had sex with a girl was in my friend's bedroom in New York. She would sit on the bed, light candles, and make art. She would draw, write, and paint in front of me. I felt like I was her muse. Hanging out in her room felt like being inside her soul. The things she painted and drew were beautiful and honest.

I was "straight," but I knew I had a crush on her and I even thought at times that I loved her. I had boyfriends before but I never had butterflies in my stomach for them. These boys never made me orgasm, I made myself orgasm.

Girls were what I really wanted and I really wanted Jenn.

So one night, we went up to her room and shut and locked the door. She lit candles and she had this playlist on. We sat next to each other, and giggled. "Are we really going to do this?" I laughed. She laughed too. I told her I had never done this before.

So we went through exactly how we were going to do this. We would kiss first, and then we would go further and stop and talk about it and make sure we still wanted to go to the next step and if at any point one of us wanted to stop, that was it, we would stop.

So roughly four hours into the first night of the long awaited physical enactment of our already raging love affair, she was on top of me and I didn't have any clothes on and I knew what was about to happen. We had talked about this and I can't tell you how badly I wanted it.

She could sense how much I wanted her. I remember her telling me to lay back and close my eyes. I remember looking down and watching her kiss all over my stomach and down to my thighs. She made me feel like she had done this before. Her tongue made its way to my pussy lips and she made circles around my clit slowly and sped up the pace hitting my clit this time. She had me doing that back-arching, oh-my-god-please-don't-stop, repeated exhales and sighs. She pleased me to the point that I wanted to cry but I held back my tears and thought *I love her*. It was that kind of orgasm. And I thought that was as good as it got, until she made me do the same thing to her, and that was even better.

We laid next to each other for a while after that, limbs intertwined, the playlist still on repeat, and the candles burning out. The sun was rising. After I had the most sexually-induced emotionally enlightening experience of my life I fell asleep next to her. I still think about her and take myself back to that magical night 'til this day.

Dominique at My Beach House

My first time with a girl was a bit unexpected. I had invited Dominique over for a weekend at the beach at my Dad's beach house.

We were walking along the beach just talking about boyfriends and all that kind of stuff. We somehow ended up talking about girls that we knew that were gay. And I admitted to her that I thought I was bisexual. To my surprise she said the same about herself.

We got back to the beach house, had dinner, and watched a movie. Somehow we ended up holding hands.

I had a double bed there so I knew we would be sleeping right next to each other. I knew something was going to happen since we both liked girls. I could feel the tension between us. We were nervous.

It was pitch black and we were close but not touching. I could feel her warm breath on me. I crossed my leg over hers and she grabbed my hand above my head.
Our thighs were touching now.

All of a sudden I was kissing her! I sat on top of her with my pussy pressed against her thigh. I started grinding on her leg. I was already wet and I'm sure she could feel it. Our sudden make-out session slowed and I told her to take her top off. She did and I did the same. I grabbed her breast in one hand and stroked her already erect nipple. Guiding my other hand down her body I pulled down her pajama shorts and found her clit. I rubbed around her clit in circles. Harder and faster until she was breathing heavily against me. In the dark I found her other breast with my mouth licking and sucking her nipple.

She started moaning and pushing her hips up to me. I took this as a sign to put my fingers inside her. I found her pussy hole and used one finger. I know how I like it and that's what I did to her using my whole hand to rub her pussy and one finger to move inside her. I could feel her muscles tightening and then the best sound in the whole world....
Her cumming.
She wanted more.
I could feel the throbbing between my legs. I wanted her so badly I nearly came then and there. But she had different ideas.
She started licking and teasing my rock hard nipples. She moaned into my chest.
My pussy was on fire now. I wanted her and needed her.

Moving away from my tits she licked her way down my body till she found my throbbing pussy. We were both panting and now I was biting my pillow to stop from moaning too loud. Pulling down my underwear she got straight into it. Poking two fingers into my soaking wet pussy and sucking my throbbing clit. Then her wet little tongue found my hole and she licked and sucked. Her tits were rubbing on my legs and I was so horny.
That's when I exploded in her mouth! She ate me up as I ground my pussy on her face. I was cumming all down her face it was the most amazing feeling ever.

Our bodies collapsed and we went right to sleep.

Kylie and Noelle

It was on a weekend last year, and my best friend Noelle and I were on the couch watching a horror movie marathon. By the time we were starting the second movie, it was getting late and cold in our apartment. Noelle grabbed a big blanket that we keep next to the couch and threw it over the two of us. She was sitting in the corner of the couch, so I snuggled back against her and then we pulled the blanket over and around both of us.

About half way through the movie, I got up to go use the bathroom (we were drinking mojitos). When I got back, I pulled the blanket off of Noelle and then sat back down between her legs and leaned back against her chest. She shook the blanket out and the pulled it back over us and then pulled her hands back inside the blanket and went to rest them on my stomach. When she did this, she not only pulled her hands inside the blanket, but also pulled them inside my shirt. I jolted. It wouldn't have been such a big deal, but I was in my pj's and wearing a shirt with no bra, so her cold hands went right inside my shirt and onto my stomach and boobs. Didn't expect that.

"What was that Noelle?" I asked.

"I didn't mean to, perv, I was just trying to get my arms back under the blanket," Noelle said in her defense. And while doing so, Noelle joked and cupped by breasts in her hands (outside of my shirt this time) and shook them really hard, saying "Oh, baby, baby."

We laughed and then began to watch the movie again.

About 15 minutes later, Alex took a drink of her mojito, and then placed her hands back under the blanket. She had been doing this the entire time during the movie, but this time it was different. When she put her hands back under the blanket, she also put them under my shirt again, but this time very slowly almost caressing me. I looked over my shoulder at her, but she was looking down with her eyes closed. I froze, but didn't stop her. Her hands continued to lightly brush my skin and walk their way up to my boobs. What was she doing? Was my best friend really going to feel me up for real? The thought of it had my mind racing. I wondered for a second if I should stop her but I didn't.

She was cupping my right boob. Her hand felt warm and sensual. My nipple reacted almost instantly and perked up. She gently squeezed my entire boob and let her fingers close in on my nipple. I pushed my back into her, and that was all she needed to be encouraged. Her fingers quickly felt and pinched my nipple while her left hand now came in as well and started its way up my stomach. We were still under the blanket.

It felt so good. Her warm hands massaging me. I could feel myself getting turned on. She must have been thinking about this since she playfully grabbed my boobs outside my shirt earlier. I had no idea she wanted this, but I was loving it.

The better she made me feel, the more I pushed back into her. I was getting wet and was wondering if she was as well. If I pushed back against her, I wondered if I was putting pressure on her pussy with my ass. I was being taken over by sexual desire.

With that, I slid my right hand down the waistband of my pj's and thong. Yep, I was already soaked. I dove my middle finger in and brought out what felt like a handful of wetness. Just then, Noelle leaned toward my ear and whispered with her hot sexy voice, "Do it, Kylie."

That was all I needed to hear. I played with myself while leaning against her body and it felt amazing. Having Noelle playing with my boobs and encouraging me to get myself off was unbelievably erotic. I was feverishly rubbing by clit. My breathing became shorter and erratic. I was getting close. Noelle could tell and began squeezing my boobs and nipples harder. "Yes. Do it. Cum for me."

Her breath was so hot and sexy in my ear. My body was so hot and aching with desire. I wanted to cum for her. I wanted to cum for another girl. "Yes, I'm cumming!" I said. My body shook although I tried so hard to stay still. I closed my eyes at the peak of my orgasm. It felt so sensual as Noelle held me tight until my orgasm subsided.

A couple of minutes later, I pulled my finger out of my soggy panties and brought it up to my lap. Alex let go of my boob and brought her hand down to reach mine. She grabbed my hand and then brought it up to the top of the blanket until just my finger was poking out. Next thing I knew I felt a warm sensual feeling on my finger. Noelle had taken my finger into her mouth and was sucking on it. She licked it clean and then brought my hand back down to my lap where we held hands for the rest of the movie.

Roommates

I had a roommate move in a couple of years ago and I
thought, do I tell her I am a lesbian? Even though I
identified as a lesbian I had only kissed women and was
still a virgin.

I decided to wait for a while to tell her, maybe a week or a
month. Then one night she came home from work, so
unhappy that I could tell the moment she came in the
door something was wrong.

"Today was terrible. I had a bad sleep last night and my
mind was wandering all day and half the work I did I now
have to redo" she said.

"You need to relax, sit down and I will get you a drink" I
told her.

I brought her back a glass of wine and she then leaned
into me, placing her head on my shoulder.

I consoled her and she decided to go take a shower. I
found myself wishing I was in the shower with her. From
time to time she would run from her room to where we
kept the laundry, she would only be wearing a towel and I
couldn't help but notice her beautiful soft white skin and
long legs.

I threw on a pair of fleece pants and a cut off shirt.

By the time I got back out to the living room Siren was

already sitting on the couch, hair damp, and only a long black t-shirt. I made some popcorn and put in a movie. I remember clearly that it was a love story. I wasn't into it that much but thought it might cheer Siren up.

As the movie played I noticed her moving closer and closer to me. With each inch I felt my hear race. Then her hand rested on my thigh. Then she turned her head. Lips only inches from mine and asked me to pause the movie. I did and asked her what was wrong.

"I told you I have had a hard time sleeping lately, and then of course what happened at work. Well I think I should tell you why" I couldn't take my eyes off of her luscious lips as she was trying to tell me something which sounded to be serious.

"Ok then, please tell me" I replied, trying to tear my stare away from her mouth.

"Well when I moved in I thought you were great. We get along so well. But there is something about me that you don't know" she sighed and looked away.

"Siren, whatever it is you can tell me" I said.

"Well, I always thought I was bisexual. But in the past few months I have realized that I am not. I am only interested in women. There's one more thing though".

Wow, could this be, she is a lesbian too, quick pinch me.

"I have to move out" she said.

Within a few moments my mind went from being unbelievably delighted, to now feeling like my heart had been torn out. I didn't know what to say or do. I stood up from the couch and looked out the window.

I headed over the couch, got down in front of her and she was about to say something when I reached up and placed one finger across her lips, instructing her to be quiet. I then leaned forward and kissed her mouth. At first I think she was in shock, but then she embraced me with her arms and pulled me closer. Her lips were soft and her tongue felt amazing against mine. We kissed for a long time, our hands caressing all over our bodies.

Finally, I had the chance to feel her soft white skin. My hand ran up and down her body, first her thigh, then her abs. Our kiss was hot, passionate, yet soft. Her hands were up under my shirt and I could feel her hand against my breasts. Cupping them so gently and running her fingers across my nipples.

She then moved slightly so that she was lying down on the couch. We broke the kiss for a moment to just look at one another and we each smiled. Then I lifted her shirt revealing her entire body. Off it went onto the floor as I crouched back and began caressing her breasts. She arched her back slightly as I sucked on her one nipple and caressed the other with my fingers.

I began to run my tongue down her body. She then grasped me and said no. I didn't know what to think. She asked me to get off and from there she went to the floor. "Now, take your clothes off, I can't let you have all the fun now can I?"

Quickly my clothes were off and we assumed the sixty-nine position. She was on the bottom and I was on top. I took a deep breath, my body trembling slightly with excitement. Then I felt her hands grasp my ass and pull me down.

So I sat on her face. Her tongue explored my pussy. I could hear her moaning as she tasted all of me. I rose up and down against her tongue. It felt incredible. With her hands placed on my abs my body started quivering. Her tongue was flicking across my clit and then diving into my pussy. She loved it, I could tell, because she took one of her hands down and pushed her arm through my leg and her body and was now playing with herself. With that site, and her tongue gliding across my pussy, I knew I was about to get off.

I warned her that I was going to cum, and she stayed with her head between my long legs. My body trembled and my breathing quickened. I started fucking her face. I played with my breasts and then suddenly, Oh god, I was cumming. It was the most amazing orgasm I ever had in my life. As I was cumming I noticed Siren fingering herself faster and faster. I felt her lick up all my juices and then leaned down to help her with her pussy. She removed her hand as I started sucking on her clit. It grew harder in my mouth and her legs were moving all over the place.

"Harder, suck my clit" she told me.

I sucked it hard and fingered her pussy with two fingers. Within no time her legs were flying and her pussy was cumming. It was delicious. I licked up each drop as she lay on the floor moaning with my pussy over her head.

Once our bodies calmed down we laid side by side. No words were exchanged, only holding and kissing.

It turned out she that the reason she wanted to move out was because she fell in love with me and thought I was straight. I fell in love with her shortly after our love making session and we became girlfriends. She still lives with me and we are still together and very much in love.

Softball Playing

To be perfectly honest, I never thought I had a chance with the first girl I ever hooked up with.

Kristen Rode was, after all, the sexiest woman I had ever laid eyes on. She had just been a feature in a music video. Everything about her was perfect-her style, her hair, her body. I considered her well out of my league and admired her.

Somehow I managed to get roped into playing softball in a league with some friends. "Sure LOL. I'm a lesbian, I must play softball, right?"

In that final game, my team was scheduled to take on Kristen's team. I looked forward to the game with mild anticipation. I got to stare at her in spandex shorts.

Three innings in, the score stood at 4-3 in our favor, and everyone had a friendly little buzz on.

As the innings ticked away, I managed not to make a fool of myself, and helped put a few runs on the board. Kristen, on the other hand, was apparently a softball prodigy which made her even hotter. But our team still won.

As the players congratulated each other and made promises of beers to be bought at the after-party, Kristen strode past me, slapping my ass on the way by. "Looking good out there," she said as I jumped in surprise.

The after-party got a little out of hand. The losing team bought the winning team a round of drinks. The winning team bought the losing team a round of drinks.

At some point, I found myself leaning against the bar next to Kristen, who smiled, leaned in, and whispered, "I meant what I said today. You're looking really good."

I wasn't sure how to react. "Oh! Thanks. You're... you're looking really good, too."

"I mean seriously!" Kristen went on, "This ass!" This time, instead of slapping, she grabbed my ass. She let her hand linger there for a few seconds. I felt my clit pulsating and everything in me suddenly ached for her. Apparently, I may have a shot with her after all.

Still struck somewhat dumb by the recent turn of events, I lifted my eyes to Kristen's and asked, "Really?"

Kristen laughed, "Really! I remember you being more talkative than this. I downed three drinks to get up the courage to hit on you and all you say is, 'really?' Am I getting shot down here?"

That was enough to shake me out of my stupor. "No. Fuck no! I was just... surprised. I didn't think you were interested."

We spent the next few hours chatting, the physical distance between us shrinking as the crowd thinned out. Finally, we were left alone in the bar with just the bartender and us.

Kristen said, "Looks like things are dying down. Want to head to my place? It's pretty close to here."

"Sure, sounds good. Let me go to the bathroom quick first" I said.

While I was drying my hands, the door swung open and Kristen strode in.

"You need to go, too? The stall is op..."

Kristen cut me off mid-sentence by pushing me against the wall. "I couldn't wait."

Our lips met in a frantic kiss, and my hands quickly made their way to her chest. "Damn, these fucking tits. You know how long I've been wanting to get my hands on these?" I said.

She moaned as I gently rubbed her nipples. "Harder," she panted.

I pinched a nipple playfully but forcefully, and Kristen moaned again... though this time her moans were approaching a noise level that might draw attention.

"Shhhhhh... shhhhhh... you're going to need to quiet it down if we're going to do this here," I told her.

"Oh god. I don't... FUCK! I don't care" she said.

"All right. Well in that case..." I thrust my hand down Kristen's shorts and promptly found her clit, already aroused. I played with it and was delighted to feel her shudder and move her hips instinctively into a more accessible position. Her pussy was dripping, and it was all I could do to restrain myself from ripping her shorts off and diving in face-first.

This tall, gorgeous woman was wet... and I had gotten her that wet. I had never felt so powerful, so completely sexual.

"Fuck me. Please, fuck me." Kristen's moans had quieted to an almost-breathless whisper.

Me, happy to oblige, stuck the middle two fingers of my right hand deep inside her, settled my palm against her clit, and then paused. "What was it you wanted?"

"Oh god... please." It was Kristen's turn to be dumbstruck.

My right hand found her left breast, once again. I pinched, harder than before, and Kristen let out an involuntary scream.

"What do you want me to do?" I asked.

"Fuck me! Just fuck me!" she said.

"There we go." I whispered as a started thrusting my fingers deep inside of Kristen. Within what felt like a few seconds, Kristen was ready to burst.

"Oh god. Please... fuck. Just keep doing that. I'm going to cum."

"That's it, right there... Oh god. Oh God..." Kristen said as she came hard all over my fingers, palm, and wrist. Her body bucked involuntarily, and she draped herself over me.

"I need to taste that pussy at some point if you're up for it" she told me. We went back to her house and continued our sex play.

All-Girl School Hook Up

Michelle and I had been friends for so long that her dorm room was as open to me as my own.

Stepping into the tiny hallway that housed the door to the shared bathroom, I began to wonder if perhaps I should have knocked more loudly.

"Michelle?" I called out.

"In here, you can come on in."

I took the few steps into the main bedroom.

How we ended up at this all-girl Catholic school is a story all its own. We weren't allowed to be alone with anyone of the opposite sex.

Touching was prohibited. No hugging, no kissing.

It got lonely.

I found my friend snug in her bed with a blanket hanging from the top bunk for privacy. She lifted a corner of the coverings to let me in.

I snuggled into her cave and handed back her USB that I had borrowed.

My mind was racing with the thoughts of what I had just read in the secret documents hidden on the USB. Being with another woman was taboo in any realm we were raised in and that was the content that was hidden on the USB.

If she really enjoyed that type of thing, would she be upset if I were to lean over and just...

My thoughts were racing. I brought my gaze up from where it had drifted down her tank top pulled snuggly over her D-cup breasts. She had no bra on.

I wondered if she was wearing anything under her blanket.

I had never known that type of sexy, dirty writing existed until I clicked on the hidden file labeled Social Studies on her USB. The erotic imagery would not leave my mind. Two women doing things to each other with their hands and their mouths.

I wasn't sure if I should tell her what I saw on the USB.

My eyes drifted down into her beautiful cleavage again. I shifted slightly, pulling at the covers that were blocking my view of her lower body.

I felt a rush straight to my center as my peaking revealed that she wasn't wearing pants.

"Sara," she said. "I was afraid I had left that on there, I was hoping you wouldn't look at it. Are you angry?"

Hmm, I thought. Turned on by the words in the fiction as well as the fact that even thinking of such a taboo subject as being with another girl could get us both kicked out, but angry?

"No way, Michelle!" I said.

"Good" she sighed in relief. "It's embarrassing."

"Actually, I thought it was hot" I said.

Leaning in and tugging the blanket a tiny bit more, my body now rested against her. I laid my head on her shoulder and took another good look down her beautiful breasts.

She turned and looked at me. I reached across with one hand and lightly touched her arm, while lifting my head up just enough to place a gentle kiss her neck.

Her gasp was enough. My hand went to her breast and hers went to my face, pulling me into her neck as I kissed all over her neck.

Her tit felt amazing in my hand spilling over my fingers as I caressed it. She pulled my face from her neck and kissed my lips. Another surge of lust ripped through me as her tongue found mine.

I turned over, laying half on top of her. Both hands full of Michelle's sexy tits, I broke the kiss and ripped her shirt off so I could suck on her.

Her head fell back as she pulled my head into her chest, begging me to take more.

I opened my mouth wide and took as much of her into my mouth as I could. I was sucking and teasing each nipple.

I began the slow, aching descent down kissing every inch of her stomach.

I finally reached the top of her boy shorts, hooked two fingers into the waistband and looked up at her.

She smiled and lifted her hips.

I stripped them down, rubbing her legs briefly, kissing

the inside of her thighs.

On my stomach, with my feet in the air, I closed my eyes and inhaled the delicious scent of my friend's sex.

I kissed both sides of her mound and her very center before allowing my tongue to taste her.

I licked from her ass cheeks to her clit.

I did it again, more slowly.

And again.

I began to grind myself into the bed in excitement.

My tongue circled her clit until she was begging for more.

I replaced my tongue with a thumb and began rubbing her tender spot.

My mouth traveled farther south to her dripping wet cunt. I licked all over her thighs, ass cheeks. Then I plunged by tongue as deep as I could inside of her and back to circling the clit.

She spread her legs wide and lifted her pussy into my face. I sucked and kissed and kept on.

"Oh, I'm gonna cum!" She whispered.

I fucked her with my tongue as she went over the edge into orgasm.

As her orgasm began to subside, I settled myself with kissing the inside of her legs as she recovered.

She reached down and pulled me on top of her. Our bare mounds grinding again each other as we kissed.

It was more than I ever imagined in a first time.

Camping with Sharon

The first girl I ever had sex with was named Sharon. She had long brown hair and light hazel eyes. She was athletic and she took care of herself. She was average height. She had a full round ass and tight legs.

Every once in a while I would look at Sharon and get butterflies inside of me. I didn't understand why. We had been friends for quite some time. I was *positive* I was straight. As was Sharon. I would just try to push my crush on her out of my mind and think about other things. I *never* would bring something embarrassing like that up to her.

We were at Sharon's place planning our next trip to Big Bear. We couldn't decide if we wanted to rent a cabin or rough it out in a tent.

"It would be nice to be inside away from the bugs!" I pointed out. When it came to insects, the girliness in me definitely came out. I wasn't a *huge* fan of camping. But for Sharon, I would try.

"Yeah, but wouldn't it be fun to sleep outside in a tent? Listening to all the sounds of the outdoors? It would be sooo peaceful," Sharon told me.

I agreed to the tent idea after she told me I could sleep in her sleeping back if I got scared.

Our boyfriends were excited because they would get to spend the whole weekend playing poker. I would have rather been playing poker than sleeping in the *wild*. We finished packing Friday night and were exhausted. We ordered pizza and we were ready for bed by 10 p.m. We always slept in each other's beds but for some reason I was nervous that night. As we lay face to face and talked, I got those feelings again-butterflies in my stomach for her.

"Sharon..." I said.

"Yeah?" replied Sharon.

"I have a dumb question...have you ever been with a girl before?" I asked.

"Well...what do you mean...?"

"You know...*with* a girl..." I shyly replied.

"Ohhh. Um. No, why? Have you?" she asked.

"No, I was just wondering... Have you ever kissed a girl before?"

"You know I haven't. You know every single thing about me!" Sharon said.

"I know, I know. Well, have you ever *wanted* to?" I asked her.

"I guess... Well, I watched this porn once and there was a girl-on-girl scene. I got turned on a little bit...What about you?"

"Well, I *am* straight. But I have wondered what it would be like," I told her.

"So. Let's try it. It won't mean anything. Just to see what it's like. And we won't tell our boyfriends," I said.

"Ummm, o-okay," Sharon stuttered.

We leaned toward each other and the instant our lips touched I felt a pulse between my thighs. At first we didn't know how we should kiss, and then Sharon opened her mouth and moved her tongue into mine. I returned the kiss and moved my tongue against hers. Sharon moaned softly. We pulled apart quickly and looked at each other in the darkness.

"Maybe we should just go to bed," I whispered.

"Yeah..." she said.

I thought about the kiss half the night. I couldn't sleep.

We got up at 6 a.m. Saturday morning. I was groggy. Sharon was up and ready to go in less than an hour. After I was ready and we were in the car getting ready to leave, I asked Sharon if everything was okay between them.

"Of course honey, why do you ask?" she said.

"Well, because of...the *kiss* and all," I said.

"It's all good. Let's go!"

We got to the camp site in a couple of hours. It was nice and away from all of the other campers. We set up our tent and went around exploring. We walked down to the waterfalls and took pictures of each other. I couldn't take my eyes off Sharon. By the end of the day we were exhausted. Sharon pulled out a bottle of wine. We changed into boy shorts and tank tops. It was so hot that night. Sharon blushed when she noticed I didn't have a bra on. She could see my nipples right through my top.

It was about midnight and we were getting a slight buzz from the wine. We were talking about our boyfriends and our jobs. We talked about everything. I remember we brought a lantern into the tent and started playing drinking games. First, we played the higher/lower game. Then we dealt hands of Texas Hold 'Em. We were getting pretty buzzed.

I told Sharon we should play truth or dare and she was in.

"Truth," Sharon said.

"Okay...hmmm...how often do you please yourself," I asked in between giggles.

"Um, truthfully!? About 3 times a week," Sharon replied. "How about you?"

"Every night!" I burst out laughing.

"Even when you're at my house!?" asked Sharon.

"Ohh no, but I sometimes want to."

"What do you mean?" Sharon asked.

"I don't know, sometimes I just get so damn horny at your house. I don't even know why!" I said.

"Hmmm. Ok, Truth or Dare?" asked Sharon with a smirk.

"Dare!" I said.

"I dare you to kiss me..." Sharon whispered.

"Are you sure...?"

"Yeah..." said Sharon.

"Okay..."

I scooted closer to Sharon and leaned in to her. I put my hand through her hair. As our lips met we both moaned quietly. Our tongues explored each other's mouths eagerly. We pulled away and stared at each other shyly. I pulled the straps off Sharon's tank top and started kissing her neck. I pulled Sharon's top down some more so that her breasts would spill out. I started sucking and licking her breasts. Sharon threw her head back and started rubbing herself underneath her boy shorts. I noticed what she was doing and was getting even more turned on. She lay down and motioned for me to lie down as well. I continued sucking on Sharon's breasts. With my free hand, I reached underneath Sharon's soaking wet boy shorts and started to rub her clit. Sharon moved her hips towards my hand. I started sliding my finger into her.

Sharon moaned louder as my finger moved in and out of her slowly. "Yes...yes...damn...more...mmmmm" Sharon moaned.

We started kissing again. Sharon pulled down my shirt and went right to sucking my breasts. I moaned and smiled. She then got up slipping my fingers out of her and sat right over my face. I spread her lips and started licking her.

"Put your fingers back in me..." moaned Sharon. I put two fingers in her. I was fingering her and licking her at the same time. Sharon was getting louder and louder. She arched her back and her whole body shook. Sharon moaned, "Fuck me, Fuck me hard." I pushed it in further. She couldn't take it any longer. She cried out, and had what seemed like the biggest orgasm ever.

She collapsed on the sleeping bag and I laid down beside her and looked at her and smiled. "Wow," Sharon whispered. She ran her hand through my hair. We promised not to tell anyone what happened.

Conclusion

Thank you again for downloading this book.

If you want more check my books out on Amazon and like my page on Facebook.

Until next time...

Best wishes to you!

-ANGIE ROSE

Love what you read?

Like Angie Rose Book Club on Facebook for more!